UNSCIENTIFIC AMERICANS

also by Roz Chast:

Last Resorts
Parallel Universes
Poems and Songs

UNSCIENTIFIC AMERICANS

cartoons by Roz Chast

A Dolphin Book

Doubleday

New York   London   Toronto   Sydney   Auckland

for B. and H.

A Dolphin Book
Published by Bantam Doubleday Dell Publishing Group, Inc.
666 Fifth Avenue, New York, New York 10103

"Dolphin" and the portrayal of two dolphins are trademarks
of Doubleday, a division of Bantam Doubleday Dell
Publishing Group, Inc.

Of the one hundred twenty-six cartoons in <u>Unscientific Americans</u>,
forty-five originally appeared in <u>The New Yorker</u> (Copyright © 1978,
1979, 1980, 1981 by The New Yorker Magazine, Inc.), and two in
<u>National Lampoon</u>. Grateful acknowledgment is made to these
publications for permission to reprint.

Manufactured in the United States of America

Fourth printing

Library of Congress Cataloging in Publication Data

Chast, Roz.
     Unscientific Americans.

  1. American wit and humor, Pictorial. I. Title.
NC1429. C525A4   1982   741.5 '973   82-4959
ISBN 0-385-27622-2   AACR2

YOUTH WANTS TO KNOW

THE AGE OF REASONS

NEVER THE EXPERIMENT

ALWAYS THE CONTROL

R. Chast

WHAT'S NEW?

Circular books.

Clothes that
ask questions.

This letter of
the alphabet.

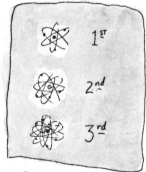

Beauty pageants
for atoms.

R. Chast

The LOCO PARENTIS SHOW

SOME POSSIBLE ANSWERS

Drain the Hudson; move everybody to Montana.

Require people to spend one day a week inside.

Massive, modern superstructures just like this one.

A nice, tall glass of water with no ice in it.

Methodical, neat arrangement of everything

R. Chast

GOOD, CLEAN FUN

Scissors

Paper

Rock

Nuclear Fission

R. Chast

MISGUIDED NOTIONS

Potatoes grow on trees

The Chinese invented the hair dryer over 1000 years ago

Toast is illegal in Belgium.

© R. Chast 78

WHO INVENTS JOKES?

Maxfield Lancaster, inventor of the "Chicken / Road" gag, December 15, 1846.

Mary Ellston, discoverer of the "Fireman / Red Suspenders" jest, August 9, 1902.

Louie Hill, founder of the "Black + White + 'Red' All Over" concept, March 30, 1922.

R. Chast

KANT at CAMP

STATE·OF·THE·ART BOOKMARKS

Hi·tech

Digital *

* Lets you know what page you're on.

Silly

R. Chast

R. Chast

SCIENCE for NITWITS

EXPERIMENT 115

Materials: **Ice cube**
Thin wire
Piece of wood
Heavy weight

This is very easy, and lots of fun, too!

You can put it together in MANY DIFFERENT WAYS!

#1:

Uh oh! Looks like someone left the ice cube out!

LET'S TRY AGAIN.

#2:

Oh, no.

R. Chast

SUPERMARKET "HELL"

They are out of everything you need!

We should be getting it tomorrow.

Every single product has a weird name!!

GLICK

TENSE PUFFS

No matter what line you're on, the person ahead of you must fight with the checker!!!

Last week it was only 32 cents!

R. Chast

WIN A VACATION FROM REASON FOR TWO!

Stay at the Silly Villa Inn!

Eat absurd foods!

Meet some outstanding illogicians!

R. Chast

FREUD THROUGH THE AGES

Even when he was quite young, Freud had his own ideas about things.

Hmmm.....

He was always asking questions,

What's your first memory?

but not too many.

Troubled dinosaurs came to him for help.

He was particularly interested in dreams.

Well, what do you think it means?

NEXT WEEK:

CRO-MAGNONS IN ANALYSIS

Andy

Jill

Sue

Gail

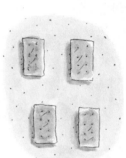
Bill

The Graham Cracker Club

{minutes of Sept. 12}

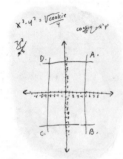

Meeting opens.

Discussed shape of cracker.

Why always rectangular, divided into four parts?

Why?

Bill proposes next G.C. look like this: → → →

EVERYBODY OBJECTS.

Discussion of expansion of club. Venezuela? Tahiti?

Took break for G.C. and milk.

Meeting adjourned.

More milk, anybody?

Gail's mom

R. Chast

YOUTH WANTS TO KNOW

Why did Lucinda dye her hair?

R. Chast

Why did Billy throw out this book?

LIFE'S HAT

Why did Sheila cancel her subscription to "Entity"?

ENTITY

Why did Richard sell his shell collection?

TALL TALES about COLDS

This guy's cold was so bad that if you lined up all the tissues he used, they'd go around the world twice.	My sister's nose got so red, cars would stop in the street when they saw it.	I knew this girl whose cold single-handedly caused Bufferin's stock to go up 50 points.

R. Chast

ADVANCED WEATHER

ANXIETY/CHILL FACTOR

Being anxious makes it feel colder than it actually is.
Here's how it works:

Let degrees of anxiety = A.

Temperature $- A^2 =$ How it actually feels.

ENNUI/HUMIDITY INDEX

Meanwhile, heat and humidity are intensified by a feeling of ennui. This is how you figure it out:

Let degrees of ennui = E.
Let degree of humidity = H.

Temperature $+ 2(E + H) =$ How hot it seems to you.

R. Chast

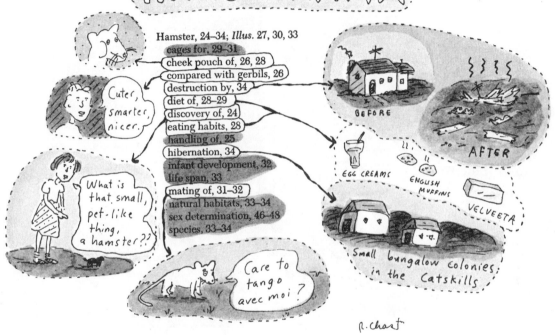

OUR FRIEND ALGEBRA

Let A = Joe

Let B = Moe

Let c = Flo

Let D = Spo

R. Chast

NOT SO VITAL STATISTICS

This jar:
8½ in. x 4 in.

Dots on dress:
172

Pages in pad: 80

Years Billy took
French: 1973—1976

R. Chast

BARNEY L.:
DUNDERHEAD or NINCOMPOOP?

R. Chast

COUSINS GO CRAZY

The night all the cousins stayed in one room, things got a little out of hand.

It all began with the customary joke-telling

What's green and skates?

Aunt Rose came in and told us to quiet down and go to sleep.

Hey, kids! Pipe down! Go to sleep!

This only made the jokes seem funnier.

HO HO HEE HEE HA

We pushed all the beds & cots together in the middle of the room—

and made ourselves a trampoline.

We thought it wouldn't be quite as noisy.

What are you kids doing??

About 20 minutes later, we started taking all the foam rubber pillows out of their cases & shredding them.

That's when the lights went on.

R. Chast

Some of NEWTON'S BROTHER'S THEORIES

PREREQUISITES

DRESSED TO THE
NINES

DRESSED TO THE
SIXES

DRESSED TO
"X", THE UNKNOWN

R. Chast

UNHOLY COW

TRIVIA TRIVIA

FIRST NOSTALGIA

There was a snap in the air,

and we thought we could detect a faint scent of coffee candies,

the kind Grandma always had around.

It was getting dark earlier and earlier.

Were Christmas decorations going up already?

We had to pick up some items at the store for Mom.

When we got out, night had almost fallen upon the city.

We detoured through the park,

but we had to hurry because dinner was always at six.

We saw this neat dog.

There was the smell of winter!

That's when we got nostalgic.

R. Chast

RAPTURES

Rapture of the Flat

Rapture of the Tiny

Rapture of the Neat

R. Chast

THE AGE OF HOOPLA

It was actually a very brief era.

There were all sorts of animals around.

There were also a lot of trees,

as well as holdovers from eons past, such as rocks and shells.

One day, everybody decided to have a party.

Even the unicellular things were invited.

Everyone who was there had a really great time.

It lasted for days and days...

clear up 'til the age of Man, More Stuff, and Furniture.

OVERLY POLITE SOCIETY

Dear Alicia,

I am just having TONS of FUN

here at the Sunnyside Hotel.

I am with Mom and Dad and Fritz. Fritz had a
stomach-ache
from eating some
weird potato chips.

We went to the beach. I found
three shells.

BRAND
X
CHIPS

I met this girl
She is a creep. She is in this hotel.

He is better now.

We had fried fish pieces for dinner last night.
Then we watched TV in the hotel room.

(assortment)

So long. I'm really
having the time of my
life.

Jill

R. Chast

EN ROUTE

3 GIRLS WHO HAD
DATES with DESTINY

Sharon backed out at the last minute,

Amy completely forgot about it,

and Melinda's mother wouldn't let her go.

ON THE TOWN

TOO FAR FROM THE MADDING CROWD

NON-MOBILE UNITS

THE
HANKY-PANKY
CLUB

A mischief-maker from way back.

Lookin' for excitement.

Restless.

Lives for the moment.

A punk.

Bored.

Out for kicks

R. Chast

THE LITTLE ENGINE THAT COULD,
BUT JUST DIDN'T FEEL LIKE IT.

CHAPTER ONE

Once there was this kid who wanted to be a dry cleaner.

Many things about the profession attracted him, for instance, the signs in the windows....

The women in the pictures were always wearing very '60's things like pill-box hats

and other artifacts that were at least 15 years out of date.

← head-band
beads
← granny glasses
← fringed vest

The men in the pictures always wore hats and smiled...

Unfortunately, this kid's parents were not sympathetic to his calling.

His dad wanted him to be an engineer or a doctor.

Why dry cleaning? Why??

His mom said she would even prefer his being a poet or artist to being a dry cleaner.

How could he explain the wonderful feeling he'd get when the acrid odor of dry cleaning chemicals filled his nostrils?

Subjects in school lost all meaning for him.

Parent·teacher conferences were scheduled.

A teacher could be discussing Uruguay's natural resources, but his mind would be filled with other imagery...

For a while, he used to pal around with this kid who wanted to be a TV repairman

but whose parents thought she ought to be a psychologist or teacher.

She thought of TV's as either "healthy" or "sick" or somewhere in-between.

Eventually his parents broke them up. He wasn't altogether upset about it.

She didn't really understand dry cleaning anyway,

all the neat things about it.

R. Chast

RISKS THEY TOOK

Bought shirt on a whim.

Asked someone for autograph.

Had a dinner party.

Didn't call Frieda.

R. Chast

R. Chast

The ALARMIST'S CORNER

IT'S "MURRAY POPPINS"

The Girl who Wished
She Was from Ipanema

The Girl who Used to
be from Ipanema

The Girl whose Best Pal
is from Ipanema

R. Chast

Jimmy's Little World

Roz Chast

SIGNS OF CIVILIZATION

RUDENESS GALORE

R. Chast

INCONSPICUOUS CONSUMPTION

The smallest tube of toothpaste.

A new ironing-board cover.

Three boxes of cereal.

R. Chast

THE FOUR MAJOR FOOD GROUPS

Regular:

Hamburger, cola, French fries, fruit pie.

Company:

Cracker variety, canapé, "interesting" cheese, mint.

Remorse:

Plain yogurt, soybeans, mineral water, tofu.

Silly:

Space-food sticks, gelatine mold with fruit salad in it, grasshopper pie.

R. Chast

DANCING IN THE DARK

R. Chast

SLIGHTLY DISTRESSING
HIGHWAY SIGNS

Shopping Spree

NO VACANCIES

remains of

ANCIENT SUBURBIA
(mid 20th c.)

Some Household Items,
Hasbrouck Heights, N.J.

Bust of woman
Found near New Rochelle, N.Y.

Ceremonial Garb,
Babylon, L.I.

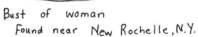

Artificial Fruit of
Syosset, L.I.

Roz Chast

The Miniature Sports

Miniature tennis

Miniature baseball

Miniature swimming

R. Chast

LAUNDRY TRIPTYCH

You can dress them up, but you can't take them out.

R. Chast

The UNHAPPY CLAM

Jiminy's Siblings

MINNIE MOUSE
ENTERS GROUP THERAPY
.... and fills out a form.

PART I

Who is most like yourself? ... Betty Rubble
Who is least like yourself? ...... Pluto
Who is easiest to talk to? ...... Mickey Mouse
Who is most difficult to talk to? ... Goofy
Whom would you like to have with you in time of danger? .... Bugs Bunny

....

In whom can you confide? ... Wilma Flintstone
Whom would you like to take with you if you anticipated having to face a difficult social situation? ... George Jetson
With whom would you like to share a room or apartment? .... Tweety Pie

....

Whom would you choose to work with? .... Barney Rubble
Whom would you choose to have fun with? ... George Jetson
To whom would you turn with your personal problems? ... Wilma Flintstone

....

Who has less serious problems than you? ... Porky Pig
Who has more serious problems than you? ..... Elmer Fudd
Who tends to bring up sexual problems? .... Pluto
Who tends most to stimulate fun and humor? .... George Jetson xox
Who is the most forward toward the opposite sex? .... Betty Boop
Who tends to probe into the intimate experiences of others? .... Koko the Clown

....

Whose hostility could you tolerate most easily? .... Bugs Bunny
Whose hostility could you tolerate the least? ... Jiminy Cricket
Whom do you consider the "best" group member in terms of making a real effort to solve his or her problems? .... Barney Rubble

PART II

INSTRUCTIONS:

In this part you are asked to complete the unfinished sentences *with the first thought that comes to your mind.*

1. The group would be very much improved if Pluto and Goofy stopped mauling each other.

2. By the time I finish with my therapy, in about 6 months, I expect to marry Mickey and live in a dream house in Merrick, Long Island.

3. The thing that annoys me most about the therapist is his lack of animation

4. I would leave the group if Mickey or George Jetson left.

R. Chast

The Guided Tour

Hell's Kitchen

Hell's Pantry

Hell's Dining Room

R. Chast

WORSE
HOMES and GARDENS

R. Chast

NANOOK GOES SOUTH

Sick of the North, Nanook heads for Florida.

He is shocked to discover the unavailability of blubber, his favorite snack.

He is boiling in his parka, but old habits die hard.

R. Chast

RIGOLETTO

PART II

For a while, he's very depressed.

Eventually, he pulls out of it, and becomes a jester in another kingdom.

He becomes well known.

PERSONS

RIGOLETTO

He writes a book.

RIGOLETTO'S

Just a Jester

He even has a fan club.

Can I have your autograph?

Suddenly, out of the blue, the old Duke shows up.

R. Chast

see RIGOLETTO PART III

COMING SOON

JOURNEY TO THE CENTER OF THE REFRIGERATOR

Here we have some very old clam dip.

This cottage cheese is from the Mesozoic Era.

And we thought this quiche was extinct!

R. Chast

The Muses' Half-Sisters & Their Symbols

Jinglene ~ Muse of musical advertisements.

TRANSISTOR RADIO

PORTABLE T.V.

Dictato ~ Muse of business correspondence.

STAMP

20¢

TYPEWRITER ERASER

CORRECTION FLUID

Brochuria ~ Muse of travel pamphlets.

FOLDED PAPER (AS SHOWN)

PALM TREE

SMILING SUN

Saffrone ~ Muse of sensational journalism.

EXCLAMATION POINT

CROSSED FINGERS

R. Chast

ESOTERIC BODY LANGUAGE

Standing like this:

Meaning: Please, can I have an English muffin?

This gesture:

Meaning: My childhood was as dull as a doornail.

This posture:

Meaning: Do you still have any servants?

R. Chast

SHELF LIVES

Happy and un-eventful. Purchased on 8/22/79.

Odd childhood. Rest of life o.k. Left store on 11/10/79.

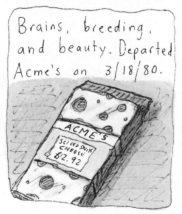

Brains, breeding, and beauty. Departed Acme's on 3/18/80.

Cheerful in spite of damage. Expired on shelf.

HOROSCOPES
for HOUSEHOLD OBJECTS

ARIES: You will have a short.

TAURUS: You will get a new coat of paint.

GEMINI: You will fall down from the wall.

CANCER: You will be lost, then found.

LEO: You will be overwound.

VIRGO: You will be lent to a neighbor.

LIBRA: You will be moved to another shelf.

SCORPIO: You will be put in the attic.

SAGITTARIUS: You will get a new handle.

CAPRICORN: You will suddenly stop working, and then start

AQUARIUS: You will save the day.

PISCES: You will have an adjustment.

R. Chast

NEW MUSIC

Crisis for Two Violins and a Doorbell

Seizure for Flute and Vacuum Cleaner

Detour for Cello, Triangle, and Coffee Bean Grinder

R. Chast

SIGNS OF CIVILIZATION

Coasters.

Matching towels.

Checkbook holders with sayings on them.

GONE WITH THE WIND

Automatically opening address books.

addresses

R. Chast

VINTAGE 1987

Chateau Fideau ~
A large, silly, barking
red bordeau.

Chateau Chapeau ~
Young, crisp. but
phobic.

Chateau Keeble ~
A fruity, playful, but
hard-of-hearing white
burgundy.

R. Chost

NOT THE BEST POLICY

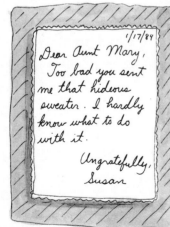

1/17/84

Dear Aunt Mary,
Too bad you sent
me that hideous
sweater. I hardly
know what to do
with it.

Ungratefully,
Susan

1/23/84

Dear Mary.
Why'd you send
me a tie? I have
so many already.

Disappointedly.
Jim

JAN. 15
DEAR AUNTY,
YOUR CHEESY
TOYS ALWKYS BREAK
2 SECONDS AFTER
I GET THEM.
BITTERLY,
TIMMY

R. Chast

APARTMENT 9-K:
A DESERT IN A CULTURAL OASIS IN A DESERT

R. Chast

MUSTS TO AVOID

R. Chast

PROSPERITY IS...

A) Across the street?

B) Over the river and through the woods?

C) Under the boardwalk?

D) Around the corner, down two blocks, a little to the left, about ½ a mile past a large intersection, etc.?

R. Chast

RAINY DAY FUN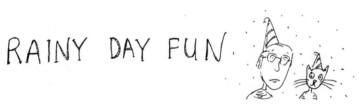

Rejected Endings for
Gone with the Wind

"After all, tomorrow is a legal holiday."

"After all, tomorrow brings us one day closer to spring."

"After all, tomorrow is Thursday."

R. Chast

FIVE LITTLE TINIES
at home...

Bill
Tim
Marsha
Sue
Ed

What are you watching, Ed?

"A Tiny Christmas" - it was made in 1939

It's not bad... what are you cooking? Smells good.

It's your favorite: BREAD-CRUMB SURPRISE.

We'll be eating bread-crumb for weeks!!!

© R. Chast 78

VARIOUS HIGHWAY LIGHTS
and their nicknames

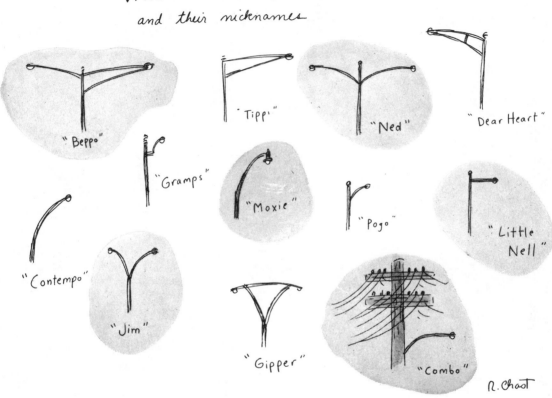

"Beppo"

"Tipp"

"Ned"

"Dear Heart"

"Gramps"

"Moxie"

"Pogo"

"Little Nell"

"Contempo"

"Jim"

"Gipper"

"Combo"

R. Chast

UNEASY CHAIRS

TEMPEST IN and AROUND A TEACUP:

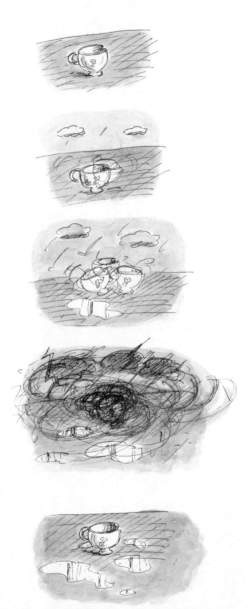

R. Chast

JUST DESSERTS

R. Chast

Guy with the dalmation who lives in your building

Out-of-work actress who appeared in alot of soaps

Neighborhood delivery boy

Girl who was in a class you took at the New School

Met at dinner party 12/14/77

Lady who works in nearby bakery on her day off

Friend of a friend

Guy seen at at least three movies you've attended recently

Lived across the hall when you were twelve

Present contestant on "My Price or Yours"

R. Chast

THINGS THAT GO
NGLEEEEKH
IN THE NIGHT

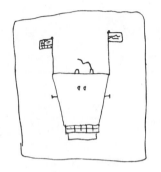

R. Chast

LUNATIC FRINGES

R. Chast

THURSDAY, 1 A.M.

R. Chast

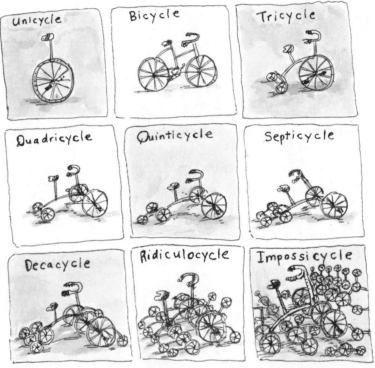

HOW TO BE YOUR OWN
CASUAL ACQUAINTANCE

1. As you walk by in the hall, say "Hi, how're ya doing?"

2. Look in the mirror: say, "Nice shirt!"

3. Query about the children or how the career is going. (optional)

4. Tell a small, funny story about something that just happened.

5. Remind yourself to get together for lunch sometime.

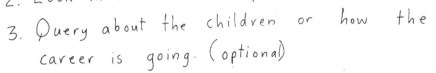
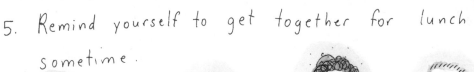

R Chast

WHERE ARE THE SNOWS OF YESTERYEAR?

R. Chast

RAINY DAY FUN

Open a can of peas!

Drink an entire glass of water!

Dial Weather!

It's coming down in buckets.

R. Chast

UPCOMING POTBOILERS

Earth's Tender Moments

Love's Deepest Fury

Schweppes Bitter Lemon

R. Chast

NEW MOVIE GENRES

Sci-fi/Western

Musical/Self-help

Sports/Horror

Documentary/Romance

Same Difference

PLINYS

Pliny the Elder

Pliny the Younger

Pliny the Tiny

R. Chast

GRASSHOPPER vs. ANT

Grasshopper knew how to play the violin.

Grasshopper was a snappier dresser, according to pictures.

Grasshopper was probably less selfish & vindictive than Ant.

R. Chast

NIGHT DRIVE

Well, it really all began with a car trip we took one night in May...

There was me and Tim and Jane, with Tim driving.

Somehow we wound up on route 84.

Around 10 PM we stopped at a LUK-EE DONUT place for some refreshment.

At first we were going to "take-out" but we changed our minds upon entering the establishment.

LUK-EE DONUT
73 VARIETIES

The abundance of pinks in the room was enough to make us stay awhile.

We ordered 3 coffees, 2 whole wheat honey glazed donuts and a jelly roll donut.

Tim smoked a Kool.

Once more we were on our way. On the car radio we got a station from Wheeling, West Virginia.

There was really quite a lot of static, but for a while it was interesting.

NUMBER THREE ON THE WWVA SOUND

We even heard a really hilarious news bulletin about a UFO sighting...

YAWING AND HOVERING...DOG WAS ALL UPSET. BLA BLA BLA

At about 12:30 AM, we pulled into the lot of a huge all-night supermarket where people bought in BULK.

SHOPARAMA

We thought we'd give it a whirl and pick up some stuff.

We needed some juice, bread, cheese, cookies, and magazines. The place was really merchandiseville.

We couldn't find anything that we needed, so we got some bottled water and organic chips.

We bought some crackers and aerosol cheese just for entertainment.

Now we felt seriously on our way. Jane fell asleep.

When she awoke she told us her dream.

It was slightly boring, but we didn't really mind.

Shortly after that, we passed some projects... It was around 2 AM by then, but we were pretty "up."

I remember thinking that I was having the time of my life, but I don't know why.

We had drifted away from WWVA and were now onto some station with a lot of homemade commercials.

We talked about: our favorite styles of clothing; Chinese food; people we knew in common; our adolescences; our parents; ice cream; very small towns; and public transportation.

The sun began to come up, and suddenly everything felt different.

R. Chast

CALLS
OF THE MILD

CONSPIRACIES OF THE

Inanimate

R. Chast

CAT'S PAJAMAS

R. Chast

FOODS OF THE DEMIGODS

R. Chast

AFTERNOON OF A FAUN

Went shopping.

Dropped stuff off at the cleaners.

Visited with Eleanor N.

How nice to see you!

R. Chast

INTERIOR LANDSCAPES

Gail

Thomas

Pete

R. Chast

THE   REJECTS

I ♠ NY   I ◇ NY   I ♣ NY

R. Chast

Surreal Estate

The Fez Building

Chateau Odd

Motel for Tinies

R. Chast

UNCOMMON STILL-LIFES

Tomato, Glass of Water,
and Toast

Book and
Cleaning Product

Chicken Leg
and Vase

Chips and Dip on Oilcloth

R. Chast

Frankly Speaking

More fun than a barrel of monkeys.

Somewhat less fun than a barrel of monkeys.

About the same amount of fun as a barrel of monkeys.

R. Chast

Vegetable Musicale

THE ROAD NOT TAKEN, TAKEN.

Well, first there was a little fruit stand.

A ways on, there were a couple of yard sales, both kind of crummy.

Then, it was really nice for quite a while.

Eventually, it turned into a superhighway.

R. Chast

CINDERELLA ~

WHERE ARE THEY NOW?

Cinderella ~

Divorced Prince; married Count Von Helsinki. Lives in Geneva, Switzerland.

Prince ~

After divorce, lost much of fortune in Monte Carlo, but made gains through development of own line of perfume.

Stepmother ~

After truce with Cinderella, opened chain of family restaurants in Florida.

Two Stepsisters ~

Both live within 5 miles of each other, with their families, in trailer parks somewhere on the outskirts of Los Angeles.

The Fairy Godmother ~

Went back to the land, 1971.

R Chast

POSTCAMBRIAN ANTICS